INSPIRATION

THE YEAR 2020 WILL GO DOWN IN THE HISTORY BOOKS FOR HAVING THE PANDEMIC OF THE CENTURY. HOWEVER, EVEN WITH ALL THE CHAOS, HYSTERIA, UNCERTAINTY, AND DEATHS ASSOCIATED WITH THIS TIME, THERE WERE STILL MANY LITTLE ONES BEING BORN, TO REMIND US OF THE MIRACULOUS POWER OF LIFE.

MY DAUGHTER AND SON-IN-LAW HAD BEEN TRAVELING ABROAD WHILE WORKING REMOTELY. HOWEVER, WHEN THEY FOUND OUT THAT THEY WERE EXPECTING, THEY DECIDED TO RETURN TO THE STATES TO HAVE THEIR BABY. THEY ARRIVED DURING THE THANKSGIVING HOLIDAY OF 2019, JUST BEFORE THE COVID-19 VIRUS SURFACED IN THE UNITED STATES. AT THAT TIME, WE DIDN'T REALIZE HOW SERIOUS THE VIRUS WOULD BE AND HOW IT WOULD IMPACT OUR LIVES. THANKFULLY WE WERE ABLE TO SHELTER TOGETHER AT OUR FAMILY HOME.

DURING MY DAUGHTER'S PRENATAL VISIT SHE ASKED THE DOCTOR, "HOW BIG IS THE BABY?" THE DOCTOR SAID, "THE BABY IS AS BIG AS A BEAN!" AND THAT IS HOW MY "BEAN BOOK" CAME TO BE.

FROM THAT MOMENT ON, WE CALLED THE BABY "BEAN" SINCE WE DIDN'T KNOW THE GENDER YET. AND, AS YOU KNOW, NICKNAMES TEND TO STICK AROUND! SO, I AFFECTIONATELY DEDICATE THIS BOOK TO "BEAN", THE NEW ADDITION TO OUR FAMILY. THIS IS AN ACCOUNT OF THE JOURNEY THAT BROUGHT BEAN INTO OUR WORLD.

I SINCERELY HOPE THAT YOU ENJOY AND LEARN A LITTLE MORE ABOUT THE MIRACLE OF BIRTH AND THE EXCITING JOURNEY EACH BEAUTIFUL BABY MUST TAKE TO MEET US! THANKFULLY, BABIES PROVIDE SOCIETY WITH HOPES AND DREAMS AND GIVE US A GLIMPSE OF WHAT THE FUTURE HOLDS.

THANK YOU FOR ALLOWING ME TO SHARE BABY BEAN'S ADVENTURE WITH YOU.

RENEE

TABLE OF CONTENTS

INTRO

EVERY SINGLE DAY THERE ARE LOVING COUPLES, WHO CHOOSE
TO SHARE THEIR LOVE BY HAVING A BABY!
AFTER ALL, A BABY IS A WONDERFUL GIFT FROM GOD FOR THE
ENTIRE FAMILY TO LOVE AND BE LOVED BY...

AND EVERY PERSON, NO MATTER HOW BIG THEY ARE TODAY, STARTED THEIR LIFE AS A TEENY-TINY BABY IN THEIR MOMMY'S TUMMY. YES, EVEN YOUR MOM, DAD, GRANDMA, AND GRANDPA WERE TINY BABIES TOO!

MONTH 1 : A TINY GRAIN OF RICE

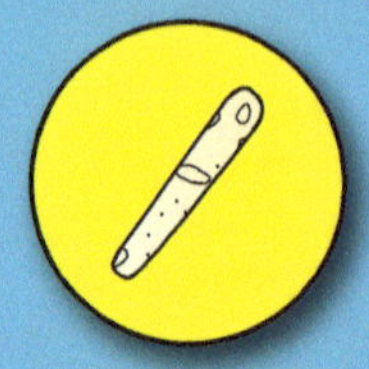

THIS STORY IS ABOUT A VERY SPECIAL BABY WE CALL "BEAN" ...
...AND THE LONG JOURNEY SHE HAD TO TAKE TO MEET US.

IT ALL STARTED WHEN BEAN'S MOM GOT THE WONDERFUL NEWS THAT SHE WAS GOING TO HAVE A BABY. THE OBSTETRICIAN (THAT'S A BABY DOCTOR), TOLD HER THAT THE BABY HAD ALREADY BEEN IN HER TUMMY FOR A WHOLE MONTH!
AND NOW, THE BABY IS COMFY AND WARM...
...SHE IS OFFICIALLY "UNDER CONSTRUCTION" – AND SHE'S GOT A LOT TO DO!
AT FIRST, THIS TINY BEING LOOKS LIKE A JUMBLE OF TEENY-TINY BUILDING BLOCKS, CALLED "CELLS".
FOR EXAMPLE, WHEN YOU PLAY WITH YOUR BLOCKS, PUTTING ONE ON TOP OF THE OTHER...THIS TINY BABY IS DOING THE SAME THING INSIDE HER MOMMY'S TUMMY!
SHE ADDS MORE BUILDING BLOCKS EACH DAY... UNTIL SHE LOOKS LIKE A LITTLE TADPOLE!
BY THE END OF THE FIRST MONTH, SHE IS ONLY AS BIG AS A GRAIN OF RICE...
...WHICH IS TINY, TINY, TINY!
BUT THIS BABY'S JOURNEY IS JUST GETTING STARTED...

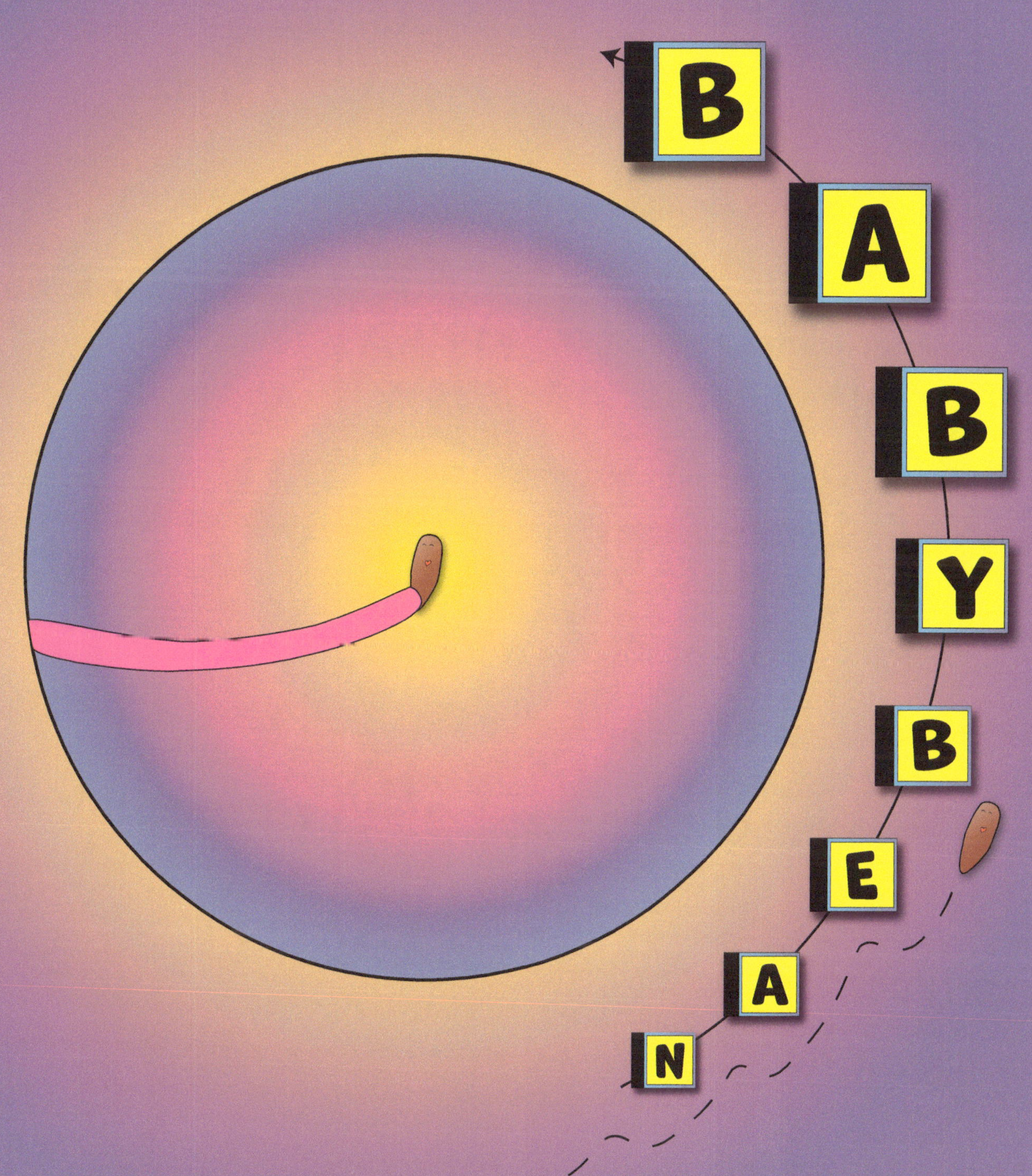

B
A
B
Y
B
E
A
N

MONTH 2 : THE INCREDIBLE BEAN

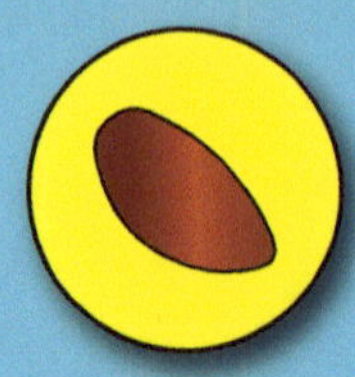

MOMMY HAS TO VISIT THE OBSTETRICIAN AGAIN SO THAT HE CAN CHECK ON THE BABY. MOMMY ASKED THE DOCTOR "HOW BIG IS MY BABY?" THE DOCTOR SAID "THE BABY IS AS BIG AS A BEAN." THAT'S HOW THIS BABY GOT THE NICKNAME "BEAN."

THIS IS AN EXCITING MONTH BECAUSE BABY BEAN IS STARTING TO GROW HER VERY OWN ARMS AND LEGS!
AT FIRST, THEY LOOK LIKE LITTLE BUDS - LIKE A FLOWER BEFORE IT BLOOMS. WITH MORE TIME AND EVEN MORE LOVE, BEAN'S ARMS AND LEGS WILL LOOK A LITTLE MORE LIKE YOURS.

BUT THAT'S NOT ALL...BEAN HAS ALSO BEEN WORKING HARD TO GROW HER EYES, NOSE, AND MOUTH! THEY LOOK LIKE TINY LITTLE DOTS ON BABY BEAN'S HEAD...THAT'S BECAUSE EVERYTHING ABOUT BEAN IS TINY, TINY, TINY!

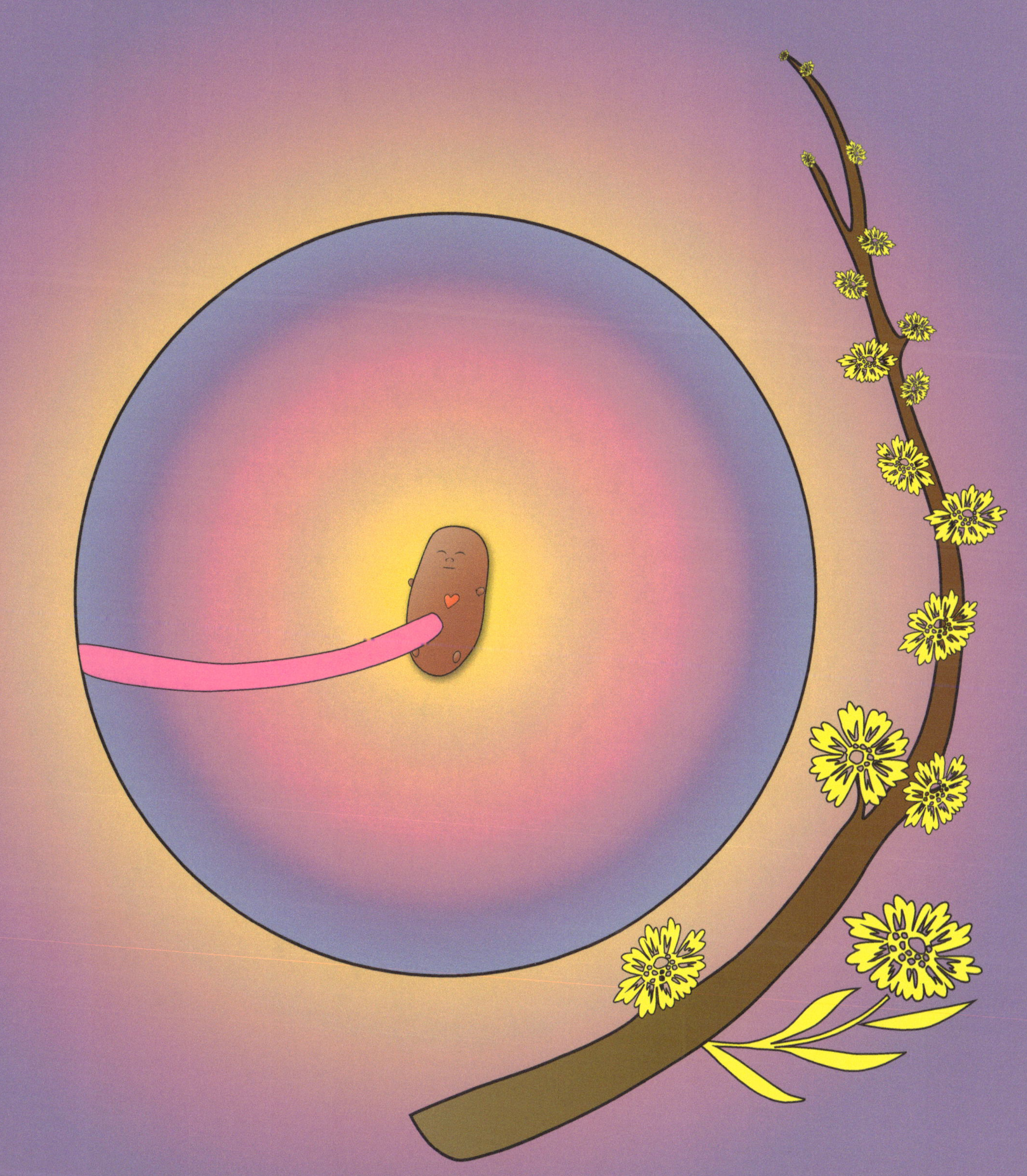

MONTH 3 : THE LITTLE LEMON

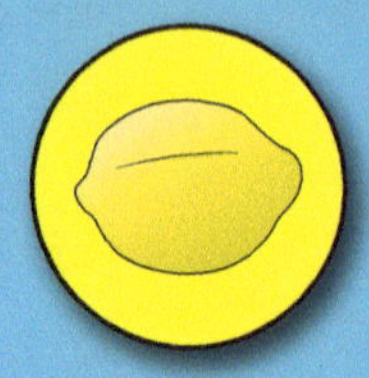

WHAT DO YOU THINK BEAN HAS BEEN UP TO THIS MONTH?
WELL, LITTLE BEAN IS GETTING STRONGER.
SHE'S WORKING HARD TO BUILD HER OWN TINY MUSCLES...
...AND NOW BEAN HAS ELBOWS THAT CAN BEND TOO!

HAVE YOU BEEN WONDERING HOW BEAN HAS BEEN EATING?
WELL, BEAN IS CONNECTED TO MOMMY THROUGH SOMETHING CALLED
AN UMBILICAL CORD ATTACHED TO BEAN'S BELLY BUTTON.
EVERYTHING THAT MOMMY EATS GETS SHARED WITH BEAN THROUGH
THIS SPECIAL TUBE...

STRAIGHT INTO BEAN'S TINY, TINY, TINY TUMMY!
EVEN THOUGH BEAN IS GROWING FAST, SHE IS ONLY AS BIG AS A
LEMON NOW.

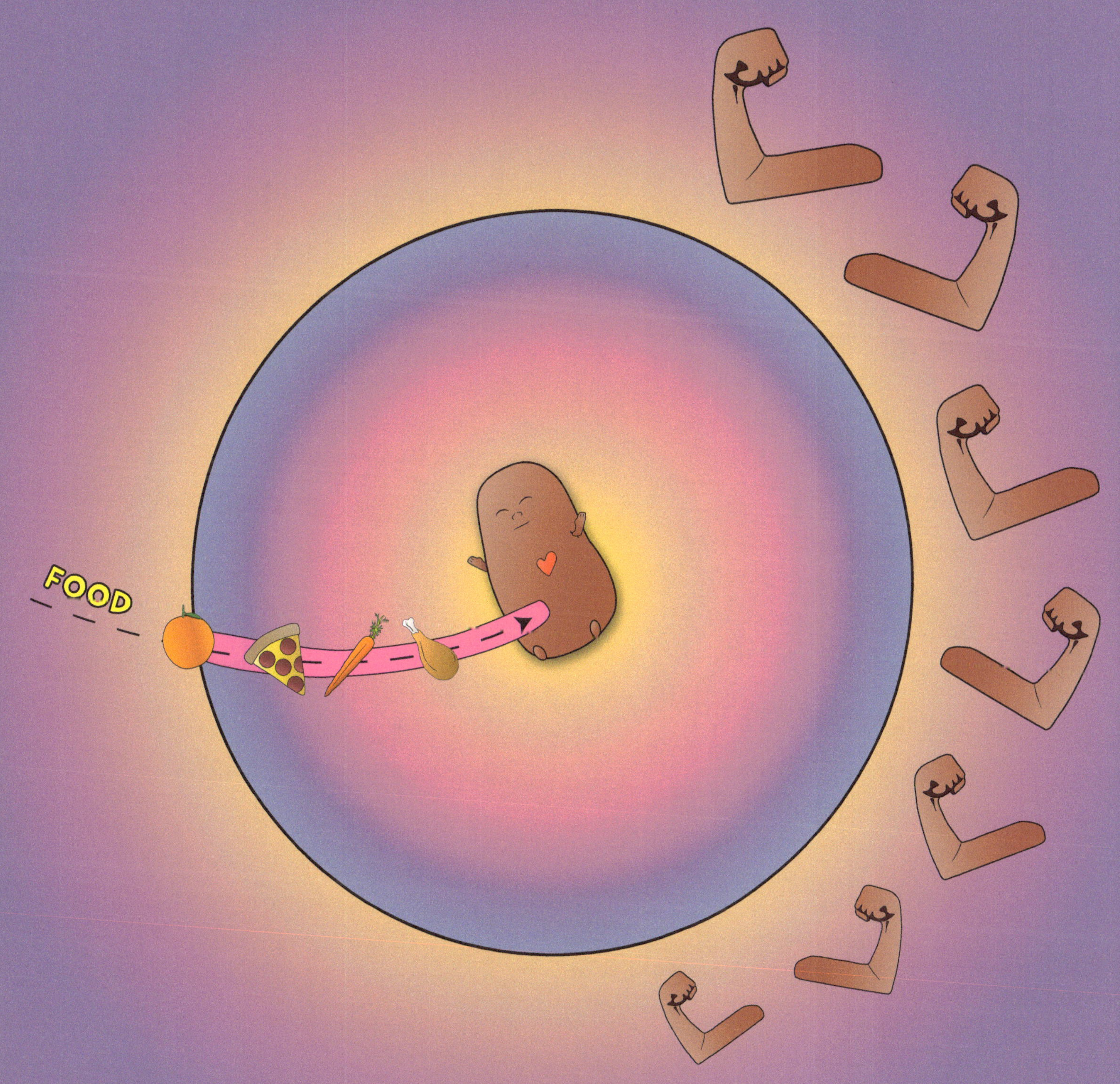
FOOD

MONTH 4 : HAPPY ORANGE

THE DOCTOR IS GOING TO TAKE BEAN'S VERY FIRST PICTURES THIS
MONTH... WITH A MACHINE THAT CAN SEE INSIDE
MOMMY'S TUMMY.
THIS MACHINE IS DIFFERENT FROM OUR PHONE CAMERAS, WHICH CAN
ONLY TAKE PICTURES OF HOW WE LOOK ON THE OUTSIDE...

THE SPECIAL MACHINE THAT THE DOCTOR WILL USE IS CALLED
AN ULTRASOUND.
IT ALLOWS MOMMY AND DADDY TO SEE BEAN FOR THE VERY
FIRST TIME...
...AND THEY ARE SO HAPPY TO DISCOVER THAT BEAN IS A GIRL!
BUT WHAT'S EVEN MORE EXCITING...

...IS THAT BEAN NOW HAS TINY LITTLE FINGERS, AND A THUMB SHE CAN
SUCK ON - HOWEVER,
SHE IS ONLY ABOUT AS BIG AS AN ORANGE...
...AND THAT IS STILL TINY, TINY, TINY!
SO, SHE WILL KEEP GROWING SAFELY INSIDE MOMMY'S TUMMY
FOR NOW!

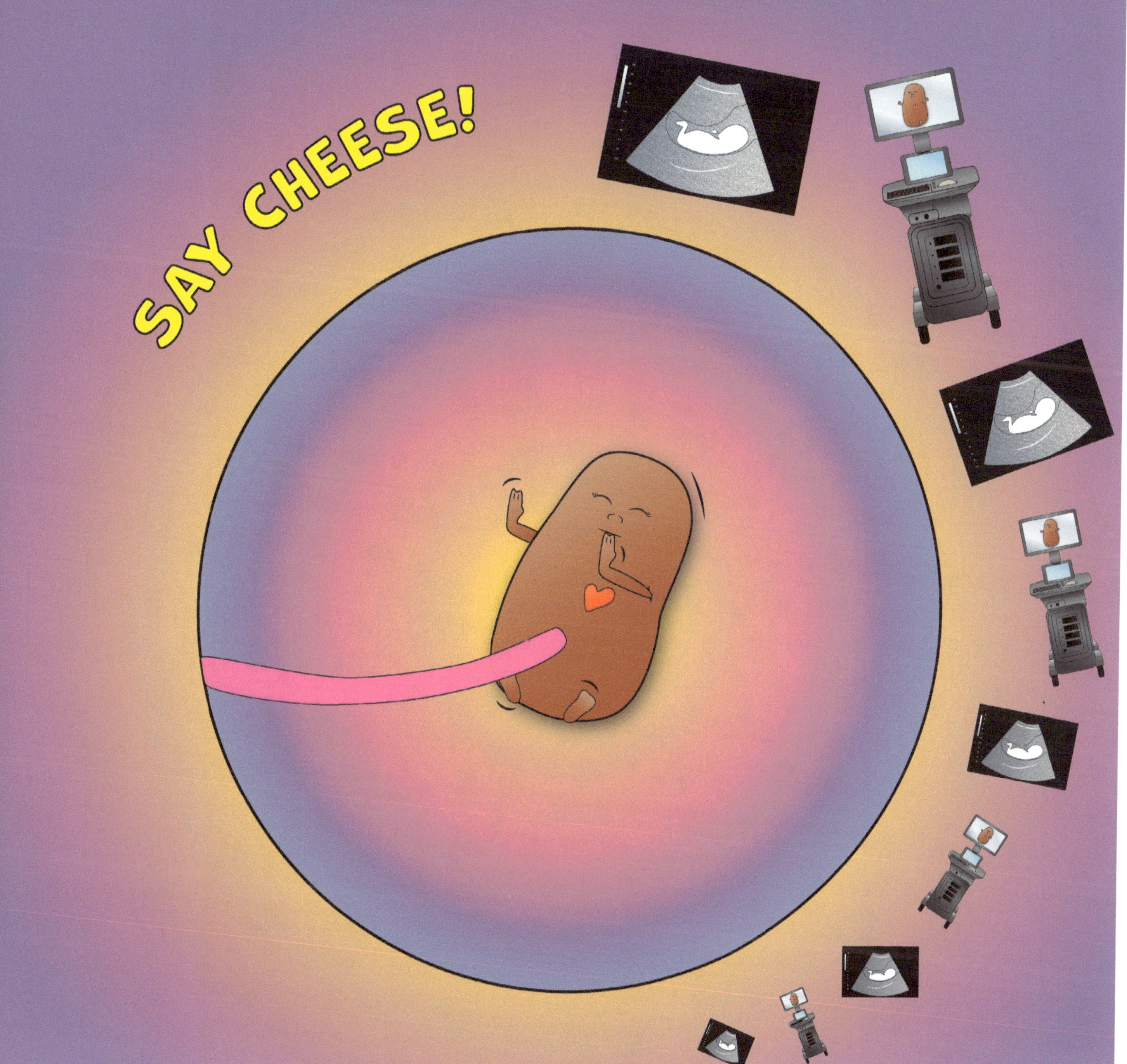

SAY CHEESE!

MONTH 5 : FRIENDLY MANGO

NOW BEAN CAN MOVE HER ARMS AND LEGS AROUND A LOT MORE...
... AND SHE NOW HAS TINY NAILS, EYEBROWS, AND EYELASHES
LIKE YOURS!
BUT BEAN IS MOST EXCITED BECAUSE SHE HAS GROWN HER OWN
TINY EARS...
AND SHE'S STARTING TO HEAR!

BEAN LOVES LISTENING TO THE SOUND OF MOMMY TALKING TO HER
AND SHE IS STARTING TO RECOGNIZE AND REMEMBER OTHER VOICES
THAT SHE HEARS AS WELL...
SO, MAKE SURE THAT YOU TALK TO HER EVERY DAY SO THAT SHE WILL
KNOW YOUR VOICE TOO!
EVEN THOUGH BEAN IS STILL TINY, TINY, TINY...
... THIS MONTH SHE IS AS BIG AS A MANGO!

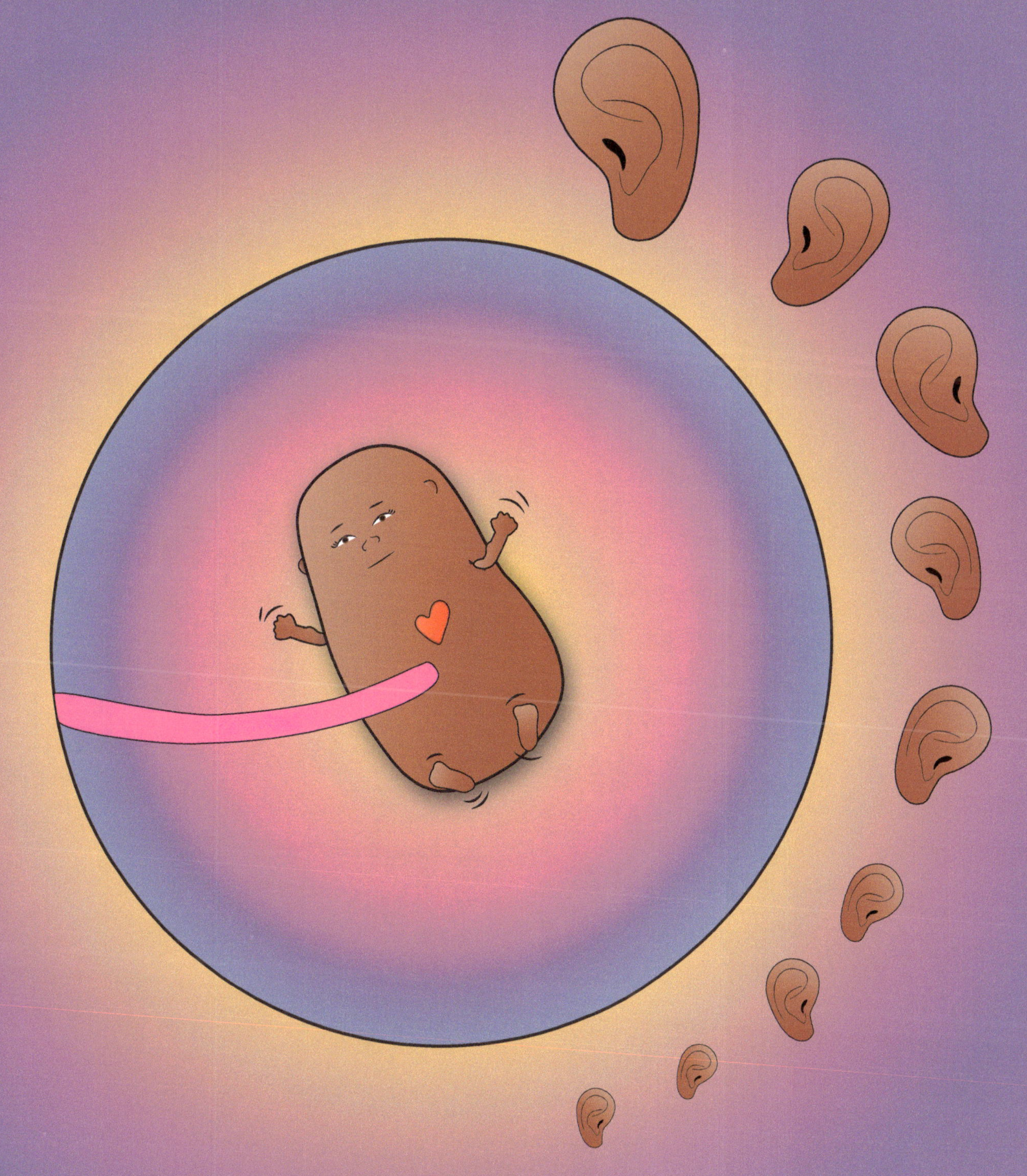

MONTH 6 : DANCING BANANA

WOW! BEAN IS GROWING HER VERY OWN LUNGS!
SOON SHE'LL BE ABLE TO BREATHE ALL BY HERSELF.
BUT IT'S A LOT OF HARD WORK TO GROW THIS QUICKLY, SO BEAN IS
WOKRING OVERTIME TO STAY SAFE...

...BY GROWING TINY WHITE HAIRS CALLED LANUGO ALL OVER HER BODY.
THIS HELPS HER TO STAY WARM AND PROTECTS HER NEW,
DELICATE SKIN.

BUT WHAT'S MOST EXCITING IS THAT BEAN'S EYES ARE STARTING TO
SEE! SO IF YOU SHINE A FLASHLIGHT ON MOMMY'S TUMMY
...BEAN MIGHT WIGGLE AROUND AND WAVE HER ARMS OR FEET — LIKE
SHE'S DANCING!
BEAN IS NOW AS LONG AS A BANANA...
...BUT SHE IS STILL TINY, TINY, TINY!

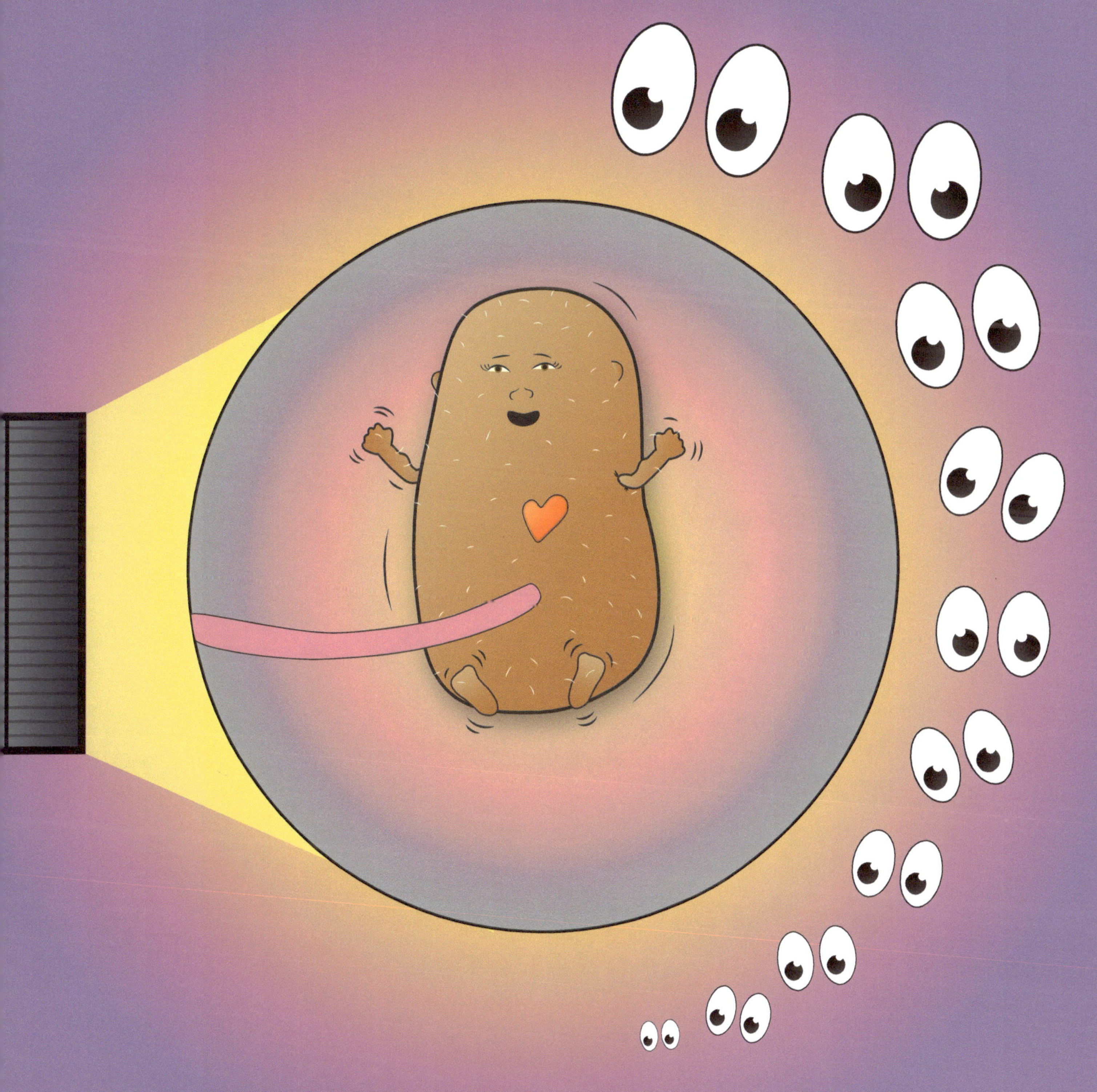

MONTH 7 : A PLAYFUL PINEAPPLE

NOW THAT BEAN HAS FINISHED GROWING HER FINGERS AND TOES...
SHE LOVES TO PLAY BY MAKING A FIST, OR TOUCHING HER NOSE.
SOON SHE'LL BE BIG AND STRONG ENOUGH TO SHOW YOU...
...BUT FOR NOW, BEAN IS STILL HARD AT WORK!

THIS MONTH, BEAN IS MOVING A LOT INSIDE MOMMY'S TUMMY! SHE IS
JABBING AND KICKING LIKE SHE IS TRYING TO GET OUT.
... SINCE SHE IS ABOUT AS LONG AS A RULER, OR DADDY'S BIG SHOE,
MOMMY CAN FEEL EVERY MOVE.

IF YOUR MOMMY IS HAVING A BABY, ASK HER TO PUT YOUR HAND ON
HER TUMMY WHERE SHE FEELS THE BABY MOVING AND STAY VERY,
VERY STILL...
... YOU MIGHT FEEL THE BABY MOVING AROUND, WITH LITTLE KICKS AND
JABS THAT ARE TINY, TINY, TINY!

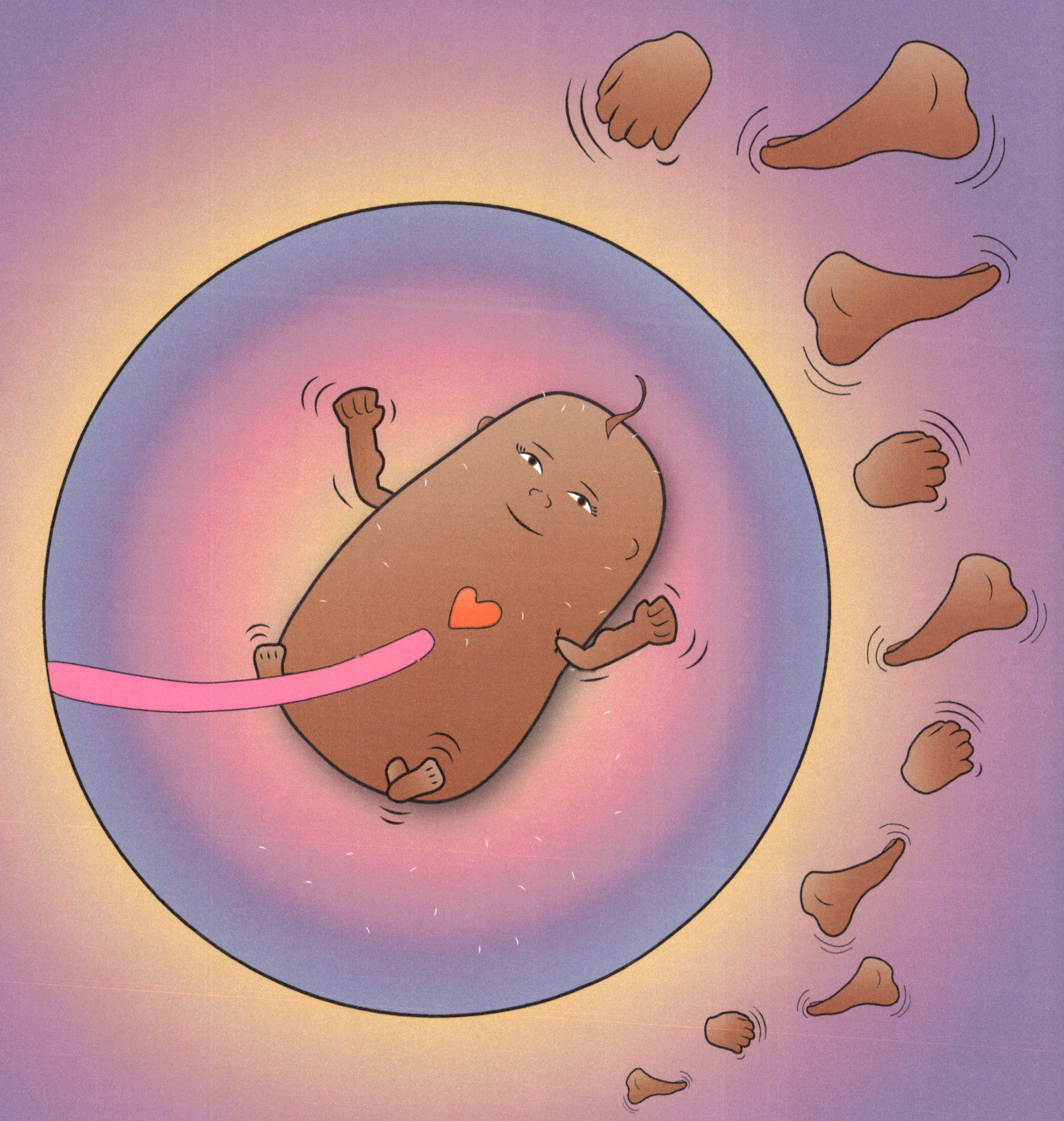

MONTH 8 : SWEET LITTLE WATERMELON

THIS MONTH, BEAN IS SO EXCITED TO MEET YOU THAT SHE IS
PRACTICING HOW TO BREATHE ALL BY HERSELF!

SHE'S STILL LEARNING, SO SHE OFTEN GETS THE HICCUPS AS SHE TRIES
TO BREATHE...
BEAN'S HICCUPS MAKE MOMMY FEEL LIKE SHE HAS BUTTERFLIES
FLUTTERING IN HER TUMMY!
BUT THE BEST PART OF THIS MONTH IS THAT BEAN CAN NOW SEE, HEAR,
FEEL, TASTE, AND SMELL.

WOW! THAT'S A LOT OF STUFF GOING ON!
CAN YOU BELIEVE THAT SHE IS AS BIG AS A LITTLE WATERMELON?
WHICH MEANS SHE'S NOT SO TINY ANYMORE.
BEAN IS ALMOST READY TO LEAVE MOMMY'S TUMMY TO BE BORN.

"HICCUP"

MONTH 9 : PUMPKIN' PICKIN' TIME

BEAN IS ALMOST DONE GROWING INSIDE MOMMY'S TUMMY!
TO PREPARE FOR HER BIRTHDAY, BEAN IS GETTING LOTS OF SLEEP...
...SINCE IT TAKES A LOT OF ENERGY TO BE BORN!

NOW THAT BEAN IS AS BIG AND HEAVY AS A PUMPKIN...
SHE'LL BE READY TO LEAVE THE SAFETY OF MOMMY'S TUMMY SOON!

SO, HELP MOMMY PACK HER BAGS AND GET READY.
ANY DAY NOW BEAN WILL BE READY TO COME HOME AND
MEET YOU...

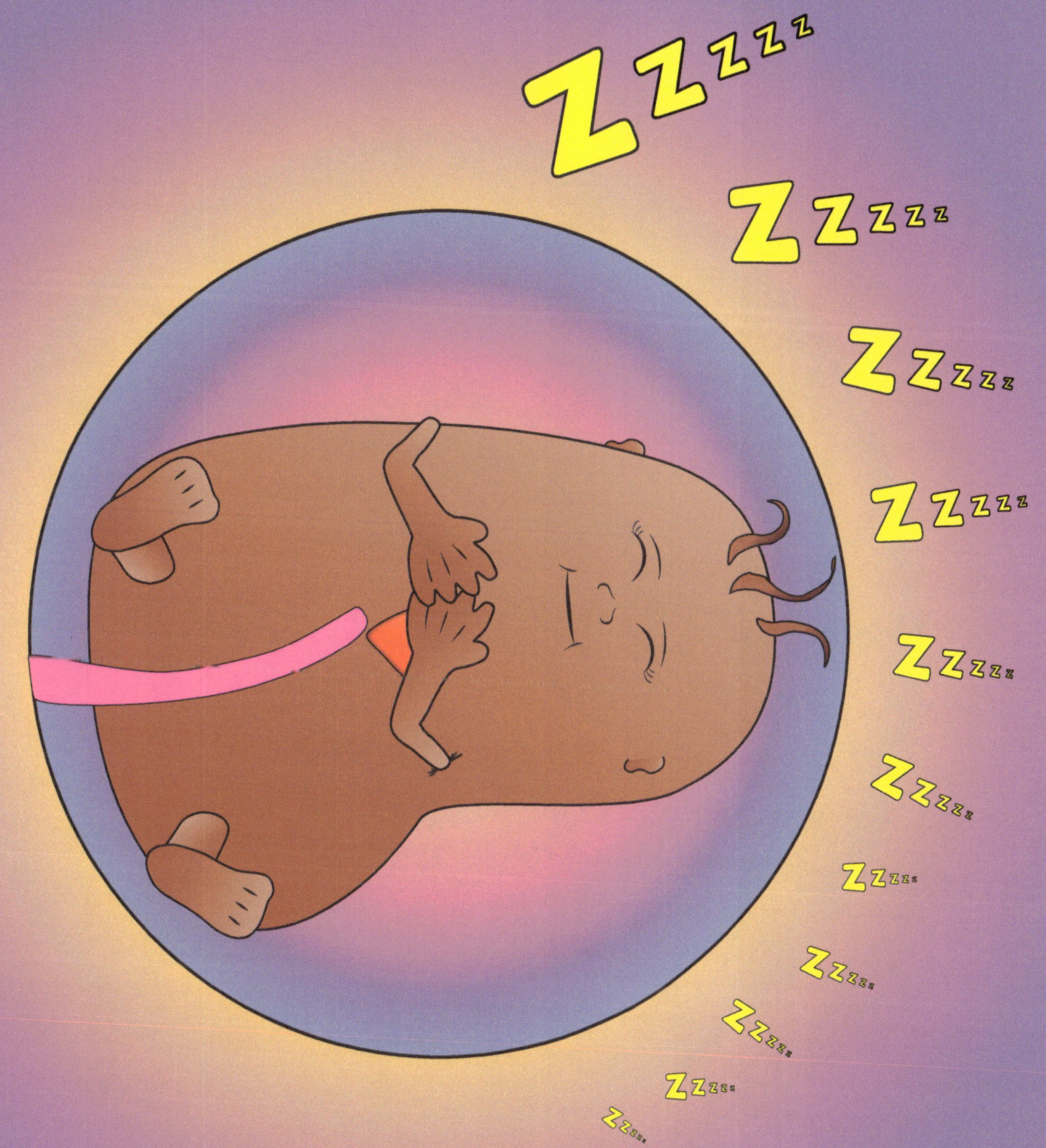

Zzzz
Zzzz
Zzzz
Zzzz
Zzzz
Zzzz
Zzzz
Zzzz
Zzzz
Zzzz

"HELLO WORLD!"

EPILOGUE

THE REAL BABY BEAN WAS BORN IN JUNE OF 2020. SHE WEIGHED 6 LBS 6 OZ AND WAS 19 ½ INCHES LONG. BEAN'S MOMMY AND DADDY ARE WONDERFUL PARENTS, WHO WILL SPEND THE REST OF THEIR LIVES LOVING BEAN AND KEEPING HER SAFE, JUST LIKE YOUR PARENTS ARE DOING FOR YOU.

AUTHOR'S THANK YOU

I WANT TO SEND A SPECIAL THANKS TO MY ILLUSTRATOR-JONATHAN STELL AND MY EDITOR SAMANTHA NOVACK. THEY HELPED ME TO ACHIEVE MY DREAM OF WRITING A BOOK. I COULDN'T HAVE DONE THIS WITHOUT THEIR EXPERTISE, TALENT, AND ENCOURAGEMENT. THEY EACH SAW MY VISION AND MOTIVATED ME TO FOLLOW MY HEART. SO, FOR ANYONE WHO IS IN NEED OF AN ILLUSTRATOR OR AN EDITOR, I URGE YOU TO CONTACT THEM, SO THAT THEY CAN HELP MAKE YOUR DREAMS COME TRUE.